QATAR

A PICTORIAL TOUR

Published with the support
and encouragement of

QATAR
الهيئة العامة للسياحة
Tourism Authority

QATAR
A PICTORIAL TOUR

GIUSEPPE MASCI

MOTIVATE
PUBLISHING

Published by Motivate Publishing

Dubai: PO Box 2331, Dubai, UAE
Tel: (+971 4) 282 4060, fax: (+971 4) 282 0428
e-mail: books@motivate.ae   www.booksarabia.com

Office 508, Building No 8, Dubai Media City, Dubai, UAE
Tel: (+971 4) 390 3550, fax: (+971 4) 390 4845

Abu Dhabi: PO Box 43072, Abu Dhabi, UAE
Tel: (+971 2) 677 2005, fax: (+971 2) 677 0124

London: Acre House, 11/15 William Road, London NW1 3ER
e-mail: motivateuk@motivate.ae

Directors: Obaid Humaid Al Tayer and Ian Fairservice

Text and captions: Frances Gillespie

Consultant Editor: David Steele
Editor: Pippa Sanderson
Deputy Editor: Moushumi Nandy
Assistant Editor: Zelda Pinto
Art Director: Andrea Willmore and Carl Bergman
Designer: Cithadel Francisco

General Manager Books: Jonathan Griffiths
Publishing Coordinator: Jenny Bateman-Irish

© Giuseppe Masci and Motivate Publishing 2007

Reprinted 2007

ISBN: 978 1 86063 197 9

British Library Cataloguing-in-Publication Data. A catalogue record for this book is
available from the British Library.

Printed by Rashid Printers & Stationers LLC, Ajman, UAE.

INTRODUCTION

Qatar today, with its vibrant capital city and commitment to continued development, is a testament to the wise leadership and vision of its Emir, HH Sheikh Hamad bin Khalifa al-Thani. Since his accession in June 1995, which continued the rule of the al-Thani family that began almost two centuries ago, Qatar has developed politically, economically and socially and looks forward with confidence to a bright future. Changes are taking place at a pace that leaves both citizens and visitors amazed.

The history of the people of this small peninsula goes back more than 7,000 years. It is likely that, even then, people were diving for pearls, and the presence of 6,000-year-old pottery from Iraq shows that they engaged in trade. For centuries the occupation of the coastal people was fishing and pearling, and the Bedouin roamed the desert with their livestock. Everyday life remained relatively unchanged until, in the 1930s, the demand for natural pearls declined.

The discovery of oil and, more recently, the development of the vast North Field gas field transformed the nation's future. Revenues from these natural resources have been invested in a wide range of ventures, including that of tourism.

Education and cultural facilities in Qatar are among the region's finest, with the establishment of Qatar Foundation. Education City, on the outskirts of the capital, houses many educational establishments including five US university campuses.

The Qatari people take a keen interest in sport. Between 1992 and 2004 world-class facilities for tennis and squash, golf and motor sports opened. Qatar hosted the Asian Games of 2006, and state-of-the-art sports facilities have been constructed all over Doha, focusing on the Aspire Zone which houses the largest sports dome in the world.

Among the building projects north of Doha is the spectacular off-shore Pearl-Qatar development, shaped like a string of pearls, which will house 30,000 residents when completed in 2009, and will include five-star hotels, international yachting marinas, shops and restaurants. Also under construction north of Doha is the massive Lusail Development, a residential and commercial centre where 200,000 people will eventually live and work.

Despite all these changes the people of Qatar do not forget their heritage and traditions, and the photographs in these pages are a record of both the old and the new. The Heritage Village being built on the outskirts of Doha will serve as a permanent memorial of the country's traditional culture, and the vast Museum of Islamic Art, scheduled to open on the Doha Corniche in 2007, will showcase one of the finest collections of art from the Muslim World.

This book will serve as an introduction to Qatar both for visitors to the country and for newly arrived expatriate residents. For those who already know and love the country and take pride in its progress, it will be a record of the transformation they have witnessed taking place, and a reminder of the rich cultural history of the Qatari people.

Previous spread and this spread: The oldest souk in Doha, Souk Waqif, was originally used by the Bedouin when they came into town to barter their wool, meat and cloth for rice, dates and other essentials. Its network of alleyways is laid out according to the merchandise offered, with sections selling traditional clothes, aromatic spices, hand-made sweets, perfumes blended to customer requirements, hardware and tools. Kitchenware shops sell everything from drinking glasses to aluminium trays big enough to hold a young roasted camel. Visitors can watch mats and baskets being woven from coloured palm leaves, or patterned cloth produced on a narrow loom. But however busy, traders always have the time to chat to a friend or a customer.

The people of Qatar follow the Islamic faith, and the majority are Sunni Muslims adhering to the strict Wahhabi doctrine, which forms the basis of Qatari law. Everyone prays five times daily, either at home or at work, or in mosques, which are elegant buildings but relatively simple and unadorned in design, or on prayer rugs in the open air. Here, at this prayer ground near the motor-sport circuit at Losail, the afternoon prayer has just been completed and people sit chatting in the shade while a small boy plays on the brightly coloured rugs.

Until the discovery of oil transformed the Qatari way of life, people lived in simple homes such as this one, with thick, mud-brick walls and shuttered windows to keep out the heat. Almost everything was made of locally available materials: roofs were constructed of poles from coastal mangrove trees, covered with palm-branch or reed matting, then a layer of stones covered with clay. Floor mats and cushions were woven from the wool of sheep and goats; baskets, fans and circular mats from palm leaves. Only enamel-ware and kerosene lamps were imported.

Souk Waqif has recently been given a facelift, to return it to an appearance more in keeping with local traditions. Roofs of mangrove poles and matting have replaced metal sheeting, and unplastered stonework walls and wooden doors present an attractive background to the vast rainbow array of cloth in the textiles section. A dressmaker's paradise, you can buy silks, laces and materials heavily embroidered with silver and gold thread, or encrusted with sequins and beads in this section. At the cheaper end of the scale is a wonderful range of cottons for as little as QR4.00 a metre.

In nearby lanes are traditional ladies' embroidered dresses, worn on special occasions, silky black cloaks known as *abayas*, and filmy scarves called *shaylas*. Also in this section are the white cotton *thobes* worn by men, along with the white cotton crocheted caps worn under the headdress: a plain or embroidered square of cream cashmere, or a cotton square in white, red and white, or a black-and-white check, held in place by an *igal*. In winter the shops stock men's heavy camel-hair coats, and cloaks lined with sheepskin. When you've finished shopping an old man with a wheelbarrow will take your purchases to your car.

For visitors wishing to give their homes an Oriental touch, shops such as this one sell colourful, hand-woven rugs from Afghanistan, Iran, Turkey and China, and exotic artefacts from Eastern countries. Swords with decorated scabbards such as the ones above are still carried on ceremonial occasions and, in a traditional Qatari dance, the *ayalah*, when two rows of men, facing each other, wave swords over their heads as they step-hop to the beat of drums.

For hundreds of years Qatar was renowned for the quality of its weaving. Traditionally, weaving was women's work and a weaver in Souk Waqif, above, demonstrates that the art is still very much alive. Narrow strips of woven material such as these are used for camel harnesses. Bedouin craft was limited to whatever was easily portable, and the weavers, using basic ground looms, produced brightly patterned rugs, cushions, saddlebags and black-striped tents. Their simple tools were made from wood and the horns of gazelles. The length of tasselled cloth, right, may owe its colours to modern synthetic dyes, but the design is one that has been in use for centuries.

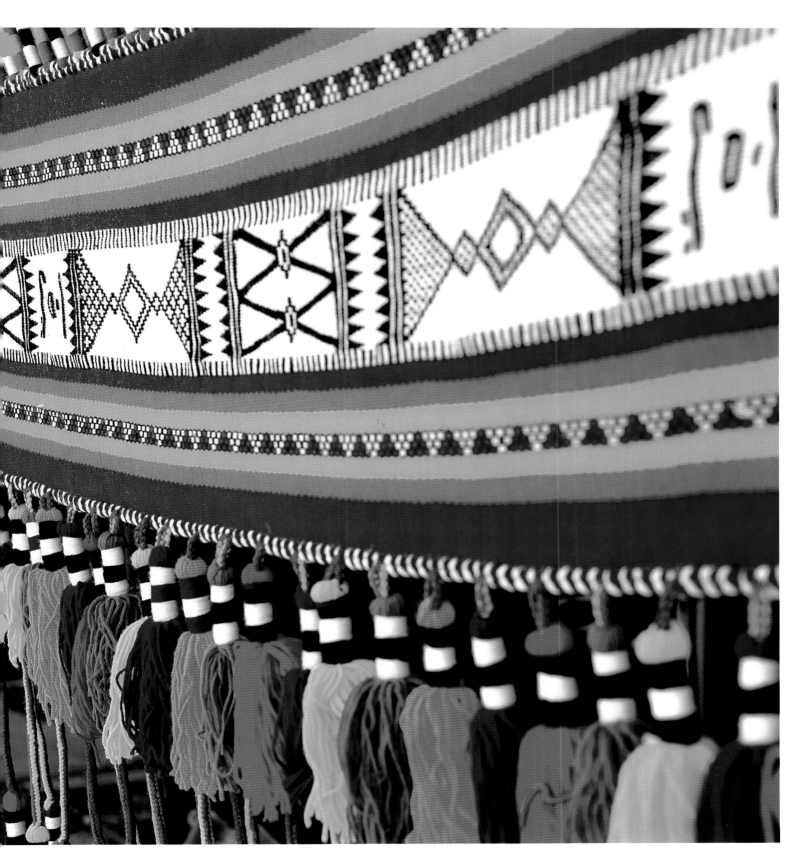

Above, left: The art of the East is characterized by its attention to ornamental detail. The elegant, curved shapes in this array of brightly tasselled ceremonial swords are outlined against the red cloth on which they are displayed.

Above right: The graceful shapes of flowering plants are a feature of Islamic decorative design, and this rich and colourful silk patchwork of floral motifs on display in a shop in Souk Waqif is a typical example.

On the edge of Souk Waqif, small shops are piled high with all the treasures of the Orient. Here you can buy almost anything from a Persian carpet or a brass-studded chest to a hubble-bubble pipe or a silver bangle. Traders are friendly and relaxed, allowing customers as much time as they need to inspect their stock, but as in all Arab souks, your bargaining power secures the best price! The raised pavements are shaded from the sun by roofs of mangrove poles and palm-leaf matting, and visitors can watch skilled craftsmen at work.

A myriad aromatic scents fill the narrow lanes of Souk Waqif's spice section, where brilliantly coloured spices are piled in pyramids in square containers and burlap sacks. The deep yellow of turmeric contrasts with the delicate green of cardamon, above, and the varied shades of red of dried tomatoes, right. The irresistible mingled scents of cumin, cloves, cinnamon, saffron and dried fruit and nuts lure visitors who come to marvel at the amazing variety on offer, as well as to buy them. A popular souvenir or gift to take home is a jar filled with layers of the different coloured spices.

Doors have always been significant in Islamic architecture. The door of a house marks the division between the public and private family space. Often, the door was the only form of artistic expression on the exterior of a house, providing a tantalizing idea of what might lie inside.

Carved antique doors such as these are on display at the National Museum and also in the private museum of Sheikh Faisal bin Jassim al-Thani at Al-Samriya near Al-Sheehaniya. The decorations, which include plant motifs and geometric patterns, are typical features of Islamic design.

For centuries, pottery jars such as these in the National Museum were used for storing drinking water or food. Their narrow necks and thick walls ensured that even on the hottest day a cool drink was available. The jar in the centre would have been used to store grain or beans. Earthenware was either made locally or imported from Iran, Iraq or the Far East, and countless fragments of pottery lie scattered on archaeological sites throughout Qatar. The earliest yet found is painted Ubaid ware from Mesopotamia, dating back 6,000 years.

The private museum of Sheikh Faisal bin Jassim al-Thani at Al-Samriya,
contains an extraordinary collection of treasures from all round the world,
housed in a purpose-built stone building resembling a gigantic Arab fort.
Inside are spacious rooms with displays of textiles, silver jewellery, coins
and bank notes, armour and weaponry, and decorative Islamic art. Vintage
cars and other forms of transport fill a long gallery, and a geology section
contains a wide variety of fossils. The museum is located on a large area of
farm land, where peacocks and gazelle wander freely through the forest.

Above: The flag of Qatar flies proudly above the façade of the National Museum. Located on Doha Corniche, it was built in 1901 as a seafront palace for the great-grandfather of the present ruler, and underwent restoration in the 1970s. The entrance is faced with richly carved gypsum panels, a feature of Islamic architecture for centuries. Powdered gypsum (calcium sulphate, quarried locally) is mixed with water to form a plaster and poured into moulds. Skilled craftsmen then carve the intricate geometric designs into the plaster before it fully hardens.

Right: Among a display of household utensils in the museum is this rotary *quern*, formerly used for grinding corn.

In this peaceful, early evening scene, fishing boats lie quietly at anchor in the harbour at Al-Wakra. Fishing is still an important industry in Qatar, providing employment for some 5,000 men. Although a number of boats are now made of fibreglass, many owners still prefer the traditional wooden vessels, as they last longer and are less costly to repair. Besides Al-Wakra, the principal fishing harbours are at Doha, Al-Khor and Al-Ruwais in the north.

The glowing lights of the ferry, which plies between Doha Corniche and Palm Tree Island, stand out against the forest of tall towers in the city's West Bay business area.

34

An informal morning fish market on the steps of the Corniche, where customers bargain for fresh fish which have been unloaded straight from the boats.

It's best to visit the fish souk early in the morning, when the overnight catch is just in. Although fish is no longer the source of protein it once was, it is still a popular dish. The variety of sizes, shapes and colours is amazing, and their English names are just as intriguing: red snappers, captains' daughters and emperors are piled in shining heaps alongside parrotfish and golden trevally.

In the wholesale vegetable souk, traders and suppliers gather to haggle over the vast array of fresh produce on offer. Vegetables are imported from around the Middle East and further afield, but agricultural farms in the centre of the peninsula also produce a wide variety of home-grown foodstuffs, from cabbage, coriander and cucumbers to eggplant, tomatoes and asparagus.

Above: Pigeons circle and roost on the Al-Qebab Mosque in Al-Ahmed Street in the centre of Doha. The mosque is named after its many domes.

Right: An ostrich peers curiously at visitors to the oasis situated at Ra's Abrouq on the west coast of the peninsula. One of a flock of African ostriches which roam freely along with re-introduced rheem gazelle, they have replaced the native Arabian ostriches which became extinct early in the last century.

A quarter of a century ago, the shoreline of the bay of Doha was smoothed out to form a perfect semi-circle, ringed by the scenic waterfront boulevard and pedestrian promenade of the Corniche, extending for 7.5 kilometres. It is lined with gardens whose tall, stately palm trees rustle in the breeze, and flower beds that are a riot of colour during the cooler months of the year.

Above: The bright trumpet blossoms of morning glory contrast vividly with
the simple outlines of a small mosque and its cone-shaped minaret.

Right: A view of Doha's West Bay area, with its rapidly growing forest of
multi-storey towers, taken from the brick-paved promenade on the Corniche.

48

The graceful pink spiral of the recently built Centre for the Presentation of Islam, the only building of its kind in Doha, is in striking contrast to the angular shapes of the buildings that surround it.

49

Above: Features of traditional Islamic architecture come together beside the walls of the Doha Fort in the heart of the capital, with crenellated white walls and, beyond them, a honey coloured mosque and a tall minaret. Hundreds of minarets pierce the skyline of Doha, each one of them of a different design.

Right: Two of the landmarks of the capital are the slender green minaret of the Grand Mosque, which stands beside the Diwan Emiri, and the famous Clock Tower with its Arabic numerals. Among the first buildings to be erected after Qatar began to export oil, they were constructed in 1956/7.

Al-Wakra, an old fishing town, features a number of fine mosques, including this beautiful example with its unusually ornate minaret. Mosque design in Qatar tends towards the simple and elegant, with decoration confined to traditional Islamic details such as the use of pierced screens to let in light, or ornamentation round the edges of a roof, as seen on the right.

The Ra's al-Nas'aa restaurant complex, with its kasbah-like red-brick façade, domes and windtowers, is a familiar landmark at the southern end of the Doha Corniche. Here, in the cool of the evening, you can sit out on one of the wooden pontoons at the back of the building, watching the fish gliding by and the twinkling lights of the city's seafront reflected in the water. Popular with both locals and expatriates are the *shishas* (hubble-bubble pipes) with their fragrant, fruit-flavoured tobacco.

Doha has a vast range of restaurants serving international cuisine, but the Balhambar Restaurant on the Doha Corniche is the place to go for anyone wanting to sample authentic Qatari food. An investment project of the Social Development Centre, local residents are taught to prepare and serve traditional dishes as part of a move to preserve the heritage of the country.

Two of Doha's countless minarets illuminated against a night sky – the distinctive minaret of the Al-Qebab Mosque, with its fluted top, in an interesting juxtaposition with the minaret surmounting the Centre for the Presentation of Islam.

Previous spread: A panoramic view of the tower blocks and cranes of Doha's fast-expanding business area, with the distinctive outline of the Doha Sheraton at the northern end and, in the foreground, the patterned, brick-paved promenade along the Corniche.

This spread: The wide promenade along the Doha Corniche, with its spectacular views across the semi-circular bay and its beds of flowers and palm trees, is popular with residents and visitors alike. Stretching from the Marriott Hotel at the southern end of the bay to the Doha Sheraton at the other, it is used by walkers and joggers at all times of the day and by picnicking families in the evenings and at weekends.

Above: An evening view across Doha Bay of the towers of the Four Seasons Hotel and complex, with their latticework domes and, to the right of the photograph, the pyramids of the Exhibition Centre and the Doha Sheraton.

Left: These peaceful sunset scenes testify that, despite the speed of Qatar's development, the simple pleasures of life are still enjoyed. Here, a man wades through the shallow waters searching for bait.

The campus of the University of Qatar contains some spectacular and elegant buildings, among them the library, above, which features circular light-grilles based on traditional screens called *mashrabiya*. When the university was constructed in 1992, it was awarded the Aga Khan Award for Architecture.

Above: The headquarters of Qatar Petroleum on the Doha Corniche, with its giant window shaped like a drop of oil.

Left: The Doha Corniche and its palm trees and high-rise buildings; with the towers of the Four Seasons hotel and business complex on the right.

The gleaming façade of one of the many new high-rise buildings, above, echoes the subtle, shifting blues of sea and sky. The Barzan Tower, right, designed by a prominent Qatari architect, combines elements of traditional architecture with the latest in modern design. Doha's West Bay area will eventually be populated by some 150 towers, housing oil-and-gas-company headquarters, hotels, banks and government offices, a testimony to the wealth and ambitious plans for the future of this fast-growing country.

69

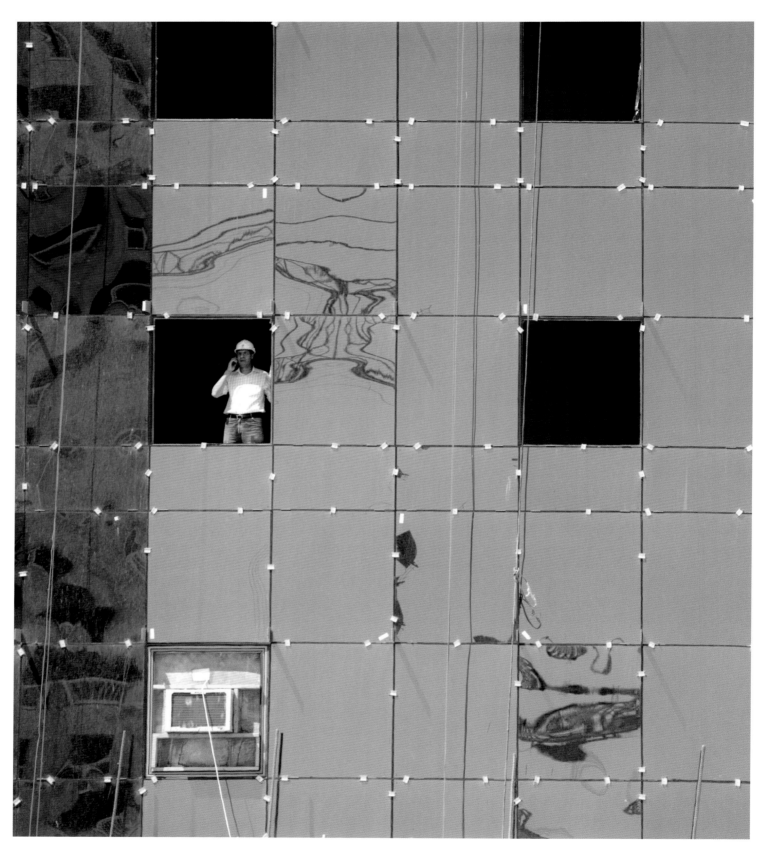

70

The construction of a forest of high-rise tower blocks has resulted in a veritable army of workers flocking to Doha. Some are seen at work, above, against the background of the bay and the Four Seasons Hotel.

Previous spread: Khalifa Sports City was the focus for the Asian Games in 2006. The 50,000-seater Khalifa Sports Stadium unites the major facilities with an arched roof structure and lighting arc, creating a spectacular silhouette against the clear blue of the sky. Other buildings include the Aspire Sports Dome, housing the largest indoor facility in the world, the Hamad Aquatic Centre and a Sports Hospital.

This spread: The tall green minaret of the Grand Mosque, above, has been a Doha landmark for 50 years. An elegant monument, right, which stands near the corner of Al-Rumeillah Park on the Corniche, incorporates decoration inspired by the intricately carved white gypsum panels that are a feature of older houses in Qatar. Fine examples can be seen on the façade of the National Museum.

A little more than half a century ago, the residents of Doha numbered less than 20,000. Now the population of this bustling, cosmopolitan city stands at almost three-quarters of a million, and is expected to rise to a million by 2010. Congested lanes of vehicles such as these on the Corniche are a symbol of a problem facing all rapidly developing cities: upgrading the road systems quickly enough to keep pace with the growth of the population.

Above: Billed as the largest shopping complex in the region when it opened in 2000, the City Center attracts 50,000 visitors daily, doubling that number at weekends. A shopping trip is a social occasion: families flock to the giant mall to meet friends and enjoy an outing together. Besides its 350 shopping outlets, including the hypermarket Carrefour, there is a 14-screen multiplex cinema, food courts and a vast entertainment centre. In addition, for the more energetic, it has two ice-skating rinks (one exclusively for women), two 10-pin bowling centres and two rock-climbing walls.

Right: Modern observation lifts in shafts lined with jade-green marble link the centre courts and serve the two ice rinks.

Above: The five floors of the gigantic mall, which include exhibition space and conference facilities, are linked by travelators, escalators and lifts.

Top left: Many international restaurant chains have a presence in the City Center, and some 40 food outlets fill two huge food courts, offering a range of international cuisine and 'fast food' popular with youngsters everywhere.

Bottom left: The main skating rink at the City Center is visible from all five floors, and draws as many spectators as skaters: busy shoppers pause for a few moments to watch the graceful movements of the skaters as they glide and twirl on the ice. These lucky youngsters are acquiring skills the likes of which their grandparents certainly could never have dreamed of.

From its modest beginnings in the 1960s, Doha International Airport has come a long way. The phenomenal growth of the national carrier, Qatar Airways, has made the building of a new airport essential. When the first phase opens in 2009, it will have the capacity to handle some 12.5-million passengers each year, and house one of the largest duty-free facilities anywhere in the world. Meanwhile, passengers are happy to browse the duty-free at the present airport, looking for a last-minute bargain.

Left: For several years after its construction in 1982 the Doha Sheraton stood alone at the northern end of Doha Bay. Visible for miles out to sea, it came to be regarded as the symbol of Doha, and continues to command the affection of the city's citizens. Other five-star hotels have since been built, and the Sheraton is now dwarfed by the multi-storey construction going on around it. However, the light and airy pyramidal interior, with its jewelled lifts, still holds a unique atmosphere of luxury and sophistication.

Far left: The Four Seasons Hotel, soaring 18-storeys high and crowned with two gleaming Arabesque domes of lattice work, is a prominent landmark at the northern end of Doha Corniche, standing at the centre of the West Bay business and residential complex. The complex includes offices, residential towers and a marina, as well as townhouse villas on the beach.

The lush green lawns and flower-filled gardens lining the Doha Corniche are popular picnic spots for families with children, for friends to meet and chat, above, or simply for sitting in restful contemplation, right.

Above: After a welcome rain shower has freshened the air, a couple take an evening stroll in Al-Rumaila Park on the Doha Corniche.

Left: A view across the glassy, calm waters of Doha Bay, looking towards the Corniche and the Diwan Emiri, the working palace of the Ruler of Qatar, His Highness Sheikh Hamad bin Khalifa al-Thani.

The Sealine Beach Resort, south of Messaieed, is a relaxing place to take a leisurely horse or camel ride along the beach. For the more adventurous, steep-sided sand dunes nearby are popular with those who like to career up and down them in 4x4s and buggies, or drive round on the desert floor.

Families gather after a rain shower on an early April evening in Al-Rumaila Park to meet friends and picnic on the grass, against a skyscape of towering cumulus clouds. The average annual rainfall in Qatar is only 75 mm, so any rain that falls is welcomed with great joy and thankfulness.

Riding into the sunset . . . a solitary horseman
enjoys an evening ride on a beach near Dukhan, a
settlement on the west coast of the Qatar peninsula.

Above: While her elders pause to admire the view, a small girl seems
preoccupied with her new bangle.

Right: In the port area of Doha, a local man pauses on the quayside to
admire the elegant lines of a sailing yacht as she lies at anchor.

Two young girls gaze out over the calm waters of the bay from the Doha Corniche. The Corniche, with its flowerbeds, lawns, tall palm trees and brick-paved promenade, is widely used by joggers, walkers and picnickers, or by those who want to relax and enjoy the scenery and the sea breezes.

While families stroll along Doha Corniche, small yachts skim briskly round the bay. Sailing and windsurfing are popular in Qatar. There is a sailing school at the Doha Sheraton, and the Doha Sailing Association was one of the earliest yacht clubs established in Qatar, almost half a century ago.

Above: Downtown Doha is a hive of activity, but there's always time to sit and chat . . . here a group of friends relax beside a lane in Souk Waqif.

Right: For a modest fee, scribes seated in small, colourful wooden kiosks at the edge of the souk will type out a document and affix an official postage stamp, or provide a translation from English into Arabic.

Above: Qatari men and a boy, walking in Souk Waqif, wear gleaming white *thobes* and, over their head cloths, the distinctive local version of the doubled black ring with a tasselled cord at the back, known as an *agal bu karkhoosh*.

Right: The shaded colonnades of the souk are a good place to pause, take a rest, and perhaps enjoy a coffee or smoke a water-pipe, known as a *shisha*.

حائل للمستلزمات البرية

متجر خش

س . ت :
ص . ب :

الرخصة التجارية :
ت :

رقم المحل   ١٢+١١

لصاحبة عبدالله هزاع الشمري

Above: Shops in the souk offer all the equipment needed for the traditional preparation of coffee: rectangular metal containers to hold the glowing charcoal over which the coffee beans are roasted on a giant spoon-shaped roasting pan (*mihamas*), bellows decorated with metal studs (*minfakh*) to tend the fire, brass pestles and mortars to grind the roasted beans, and the brass coffee pots (*dallah*) in which the coffee is finally prepared. The local variety of coffee has pounded cardamom seeds added to the brew.

Left: Cobblers in Souk Waqif, sitting in their tiny lock-up booths, will quickly fix a broken sandal or re-sole a shoe, while the customer sits and waits.

When this elderly gentleman, left, was young, Doha was a little town of modest one and two-storey, mud-brick or coral buildings, crowded together along narrow lanes (*sikkas*) and extending only a few-hundred metres inland from the bay. In just a few decades revenue from the export of oil and liquified natural gas has transformed it into a 21st-century metropolis. These two young citizens, above, immaculate in their crisp white *thobes* and caps (*keffiyas*), know nothing of that vanished world 'before the oil came'.

Some of the many faces belonging to the cosmopolitan city of Doha. Above, an elderly Qatari citizen, while, top right, Filipino construction workers and others in the City Center pause to watch skaters on the ice rink. Below right, one of the 5,000 fishermen, most of whom hail from India.

Workers from Pakistan at the wholesale fruit and vegetable souk near the Salwa Road in Doha. The man on the right has dyed his beard with henna.

This smiling lady is one of many nationalities who enjoy a gentle evening stroll along the popular Doha Corniche.

A symphony in yellow created by a lady on the access ramp to the spectator gallery at Losail International Circuit, a few kilometres north of Doha.

Falconry has a long history in Qatar, ever since the days when falcons were used by the Bedouin for hunting houbara bustards and hares, and it is still an important part of Qatari culture. There is a falcon souk, and a number of shops such as this one in Souk Waqif, where hooded peregrine and saker falcons sit quietly on their Astroturf perches. Female birds, being larger and more powerful, are preferred, and the finest can change hands for thousands of riyals. Wild birds migrating to Qatar are trapped along the coast, but many falcons are imported and hunting, which lasts from October to March, takes place both in Qatar and abroad.

Identifying features of the Arabian horse are the wedge-shaped head, narrow muzzle, large, beautiful eyes set wide apart, and the tail carried high. One of the oldest and purest breeds, the Arabian was bred to travel swiftly over long distances, needing only limited food and water. Qatar has some of the finest pure-bred Arab horses in the world, and the Al-Shaqab Stud Farm, owned by HH the Emir, was one of the first private studs to be established in the Arabian Gulf. Horse racing and endurance racing are popular, and the involvement of the ruling family ensures Qatar's place in the equestrian world.

For centuries, the Bedouin used camels, not only as pack animals but also for their milk, meat, hides and hair. Today, camels are still much-prized animals and herds of milk camels can be seen grazing all over the desert, but it is the racing camels which attract most attention. They can be seen exercising on the road-side tracks, above, at Al-Sheehaniya, a small inland town 30-minutes' drive from Doha, where camel racing takes place. The races are keenly followed, with the best camels changing hands for the same astronomical sums as race horses. High-tech robots have now replaced the young jockeys, and visitors to the races, which take place between October and April, are welcome. There is a grandstand, but owners usually prefer to race alongside the track in their 4x4s, urging on the camels.

A trainer with his camels, wearing their knitted, rainbow-coloured nose covers. Traditionally, racing camels were fed on honey, dates, alfalfa and milk. Nowadays they can enjoy special formula pellets as well.

Above: The clubhouse at the Doha Golf Club incorporates traditional Arabic architectural features. The club was opened in 1996 and, every year since 1998, the world's top golfers have gathered for the two-million US dollar Qatar Masters Championship. Its 18-hole course, one of the longest on the PGA tour, is superbly landscaped with lakes, giant cacti, palm trees, and rock formations, the lush greenery contrasting with the barren desert all around.

Top right: The course is a haven for wildlife, including the ducks which sometimes stroll on the links: just one of the hazards encountered by golfers!

Below right: One of the eight beautiful lakes along the course, home to aquatic life including fish, frogs and water birds.

119

Surrounded by more than 500 kilometres of coastline, Qatar is home to a wide variety of water sports. Kite surfing, above, is a relatively new sport in the region, but jet skiing, right, has been popular for a number of years, and local championships attract competitors from around the world.

The oval ice rink in the City Center mall has been used for Friday morning ice-hockey matches since October 2003, attracting large numbers of spectators who come to watch this exciting, fast-moving sport. There are currently five teams in the Qatar International Ice Hockey League and matches are played against other Gulf teams, as well as those from further afield.

Riders head for the starting line, above, at the Losail International Circuit on the northern outskirts of Doha. In 2006, for the first time in the Middle East, the first leg of the Grand Prix Masters series was held here. Constructed in 2003/4, the circuit drew praise at the inaugural event of October 2004, the Marlboro Grand Prix, for its impressive safety standards and facilities. The races attract widespread media coverage, right, and crowds of spectators, although for one young fan the noise is all just a little too much!

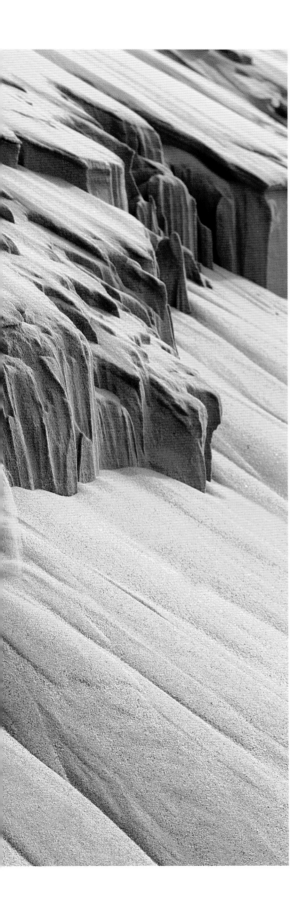

Above: Near the Sealine Beach Resort at Mesaieed, where the long stretch of dunes begins, enthusiastic young riders drive up and down the slopes.

Left: One of the most spectacular landscapes in the entire Arabian Gulf is in southern Qatar, where majestic dunes of golden sand form crescent-shaped *barchans* and long, undulating ridges known as *seif* dunes. Driven by the prevailing winds, they drift slowly down to the shallow tidal lagoon of Khor al-Adaid, the Inland Sea. A trip to this uniquely beautiful region, with its sparkling blue water fringed by the towering dunes, is a must.

On Qatar's southern border, the Khor al-Adaid is one of the most beautiful areas in the country. It features mile upon mile of golden beaches, and stunning views across turquoise blue, shimmering waters, where dolphins play, ospreys hunt for fish and flocks of flamingoes feed in the shallows, to the pink, ridged, rocky hills of Saudi Arabia on the far side. At weekends the beaches are the venue for day trippers and campers, but the area is so large it is often possible to have a perfect beach all to yourself. Dune driving is popular here, but best undertaken by experienced drivers.

At Al-Khor, Qatar's second city, the principal sources of income before the oil era, fishing and pearling, are commemorated at the Dhow Monument. Diesel engines replaced sails half a century ago, but the fishing dhows that crowd the harbour at Al-Khor, and at Al-Thakira on the northern end of Khor Bay, are built in the same traditional style recognisable all over the Gulf region.

A view of the tranquil beach along the Corniche at Al-Khor, where a small dhow is the main feature of the children's playground.

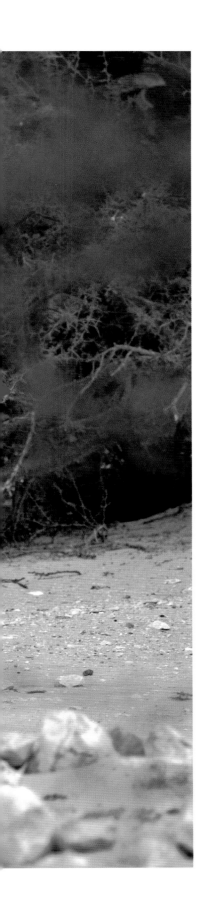

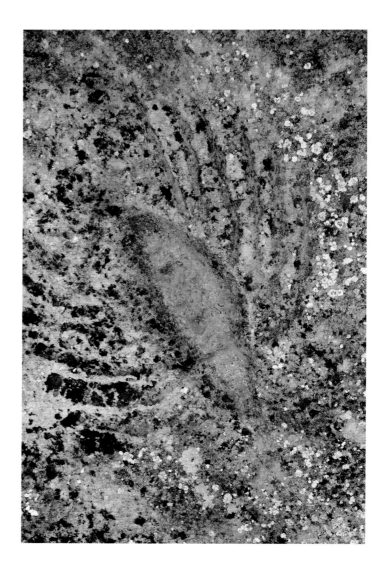

Previous spread: The delicate rheem, or sand gazelle, left, was hunted to extinction in the wild in Qatar in the 1950s, but survived in several breeding herds maintained by the government, and in private collections. Recently released at Ra's Abrouq on the west coast, these delicate animals can once again be seen wandering the sand and gravel plains. Qatar pioneered the conservation of the Arabian oryx, right, a large and strikingly beautiful cream-coloured antelope with long horns and a black-patterned face that some believe gave rise to the legend of the unicorn. The oryx is also frequently used as symbol in heraldry. Once threatened with extinction, this graceful animal now thrives in several herds around the country, and there are plans to re-introduce it into the wild. The main breeding herd is at a reserve at Al-Sheehaniya, where visits can be arranged by tour agencies.

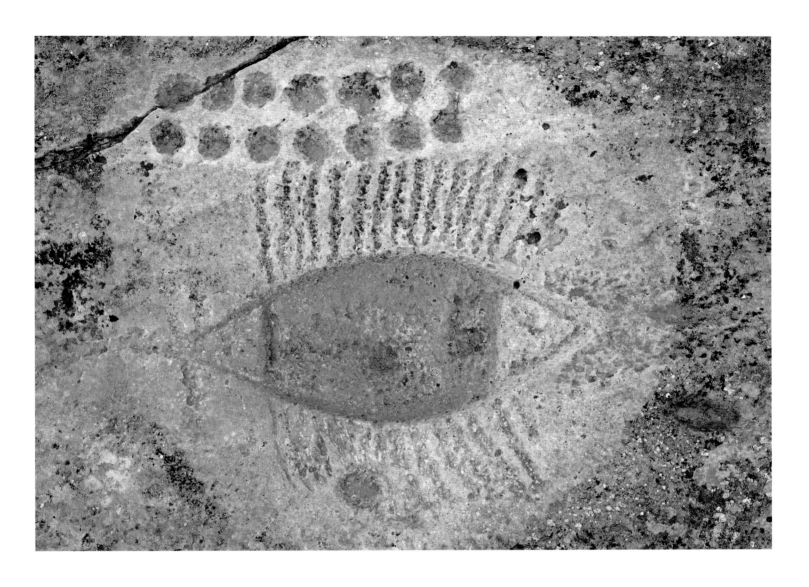

This spread: These mysterious carvings of oared boats, trailing metal or triangular stone anchors and carrying a steering oar, above, seem to crawl like scorpions across the grey, weathered limestone rocks at Jabal al-Jassasiya, 45 minutes' drive north of Doha. The date of these petroglyphs is not known, but boats with oars were in use for centuries on the pearling banks. Carvings like these have not been found anywhere else in the Gulf region. Elsewhere on these rocks are side views of large merchant vessels, some showing European influences on local ship design. Hundreds of double rows, circular 'rosettes' and linked pairs of shallow holes, perhaps used for games involving counters, are scattered over the surface of the limestone, left. Similar configurations of holes, called 'cup marks', can be seen at several other low-lying rocky locations around the north-east and north-west coast.

The large village of Umm Slal Mohammed lies about 20 kilometres north of Doha and is dominated by the tall towers and crenellated walls of a fortified residence built in 1910 by Sheikh Mohammed bin Jassim bin Thani al-Thani, a grandson of the founder of the al-Thani dynasty in Qatar. The view taken on the roof of the building, left, shows one of the towers which were used for surveillance. The village has a good supply of water and, as seen in the above photograph, is surrounded by extensive date gardens and farms.

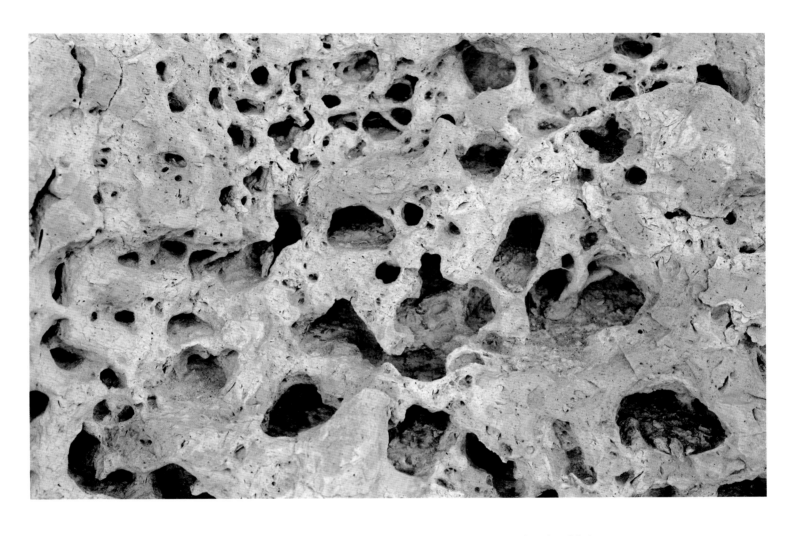

Pages 138–143: Bordering the western coastline on the peninsula of Ra's Abrouq are plateaux of gleaming white limestone. Over time, wind-blown sand has scoured and honed the edges of the platforms into strange shapes: spindly pinnacles; giant, free-standing mushrooms and arches worn right through the rock. They rise above the drifting sand of the desert floor like the remains of an ancient landscape. Here and there on the plateaux, known as 'mesas', lie stone tools left by the earliest human beings to live in the area now known as Qatar, which date back some 8,000 years.

The opening ceremony at the Asian Games 2006 in Doha was impressive, with vibrant fireworks and colourful displays. It embodied the winning spirit of the Qatari athletes, who won 32 medals with nine gold and 12 silver. It was one of the largest Asian games ever, both in terms of sporting achievement and planning, transforming Doha into an international capital.